The Toddlers Songbook

Stories written by
V. Gilbert Beers

Concept and music by
Ellen Banks Elwell

Illustrated by
Carole Boerke

Chariot Books is an imprint of ChariotVictor Publishing,
a division of Cook Communications, Colorado Springs, Colorado 80918
Cook Communications, Paris, Ontario
Kingsway Communications, Eastbourne, England

Musical arrangements © 1994, Ellen Banks Elwell

Illustrations © 1994 by Educational Publishing Concepts, Inc., Wheaton, Illinois.

Text © 1994, V. Gilbert Beers.

All rights reserved. Written permission must be secured from the publisher to use or reproduce any part of this book, except for brief quotations in critical reviews or articles.

ISBN 1-56476-300-5

Printed in Canada

4 5 6 7 8 9 10 Printing / Year 98 97

Credits

Author:	V. Gilbert Beers
Illustrator:	Carole Boerke
Executive Producer:	Ellen Banks Elwell
Producer/Arranger:	Larry Shackley
Track Arrangements and production:	Larry Shackley
Written Arrangements:	Ellen Banks Elwell
Piano/Synthesizer/Drum Programming:	Larry Shackley
Violin/Cello/French Horn arrangements:	Ellen Banks Elwell
Vocal Director:	Ellen Banks Elwell
Adult Vocal Soloist:	Gail Pflederer
Youth Vocals:	Lisa Couture, Nathan Elwell, Jaimee Harbeck, Jeff Harbeck, Julee Harbeck, Kim Huizingh, Beth Liebenow, Sarah Meyer, Ashley Petti, Josh Reynolds, Lucy Sullivan
Violin:	Gail Salvatori
Cello:	Kathy Beers Cathey
French Horn:	Steve Pierson

Vocals/Instruments/Piano recorded at Jor-Dan Studios, Wheaton, Illinois
Engineer: Glen West
Assistant: Andy Kuharich

Synthesizer tracks recorded and project mixed at Moody Broadcasting, Chicago, Illinois
Engineer: Joe Carlson

Mastered at Jor-Dan Studios, Wheaton, Illinois
Engineer: Glen West
Assistant: Andy Kuharich

Contents

Songs

IF YOU'RE HAPPY	6
PRAISE HIM, PRAISE HIM	12
OLD MACDONALD	20
RISE AND SHINE	28
TWINKLE, TWINKLE, LITTLE STAR	30
WHO DID?	36
MARY HAD A LITTLE LAMB	44
GOD IS SO GOOD	52
EENSY WEENSY SPIDER	60
MARY HAD A BABY	68
MOZART'S LULLABY	76
HE'S GOT THE WHOLE WORLD IN HIS HANDS	84

Stories

If You're Happy	8
Praise Him	14
Old MacDonald	22
Twinkle, Twinkle, Little Star	32
Who Swallowed Jonah?	38
Mary Had a Little Lamb	46
God Is So Good	54
Eensy Weensy Spider	62
Mary Had a Baby	70
Mozart's Lullaby	78
He's Got the Whole World In His Hands	86

Songs

ARE YOU SLEEPING?............92
JESUS LOVES ME....................94
SIX LITTLE DUCKS...............102
ZACCHAEUS 110
OH, HOW LOVELY
IS THE EVENING...................118
ALL THROUGH
THE NIGHT............................126
HERE WE GO 'ROUND
THE MULBERRY BUSH.......134
HALLELU, HALLELU..........142
LITTLE BOY BLUE................144
OH, BE CAREFUL 146
I LOVE LITTLE KITTY 154
LITTLE DAVID, PLAY
ON YOUR HARP...................161

Stories

Jesus Loves Me 96
Six Little Ducks 104
Zacchaeus 112
Oh, How Lovely
Is the Evening 120

All Through the Night 128
Here We Go 'Round the
Mulberry Bush........................136

Oh, Be Careful 148
I Love Little Kitty...................156
Little David, Play on
Your Harp................................164

IF YOU'RE HAPPY

vs. 2 If you're happy and you know it, stomp your feet . . .
vs. 3 If you're happy and you know it, say Amen! . . .

If You're Happy

Are you happy? Do you know it?
Clap your hands!
Thank You, God!

Are you happy? Do you know it?
Stomp your feet!
Thank You, God!

Are you happy? Do you know it?
Shout AMEN!
Thank You, God!

Are you happy? Do you know it?
Clap your hands, stomp your feet, shout AMEN!
Thank You, God!

PRAISE HIM, PRAISE HIM

vs. 2 Thank Him, thank Him . . .
vs. 3 Serve Him, serve Him . . .

Praise Him

I will praise
You, God,
for loving me.
I will praise You
for my warm
clothing.

I will praise You, God,
for loving me.
I will praise You for my
good food.

I will thank You, God, for loving me.

I will thank You for my good house and warm bed.

I will serve You, God, because You love me.
I will serve You by doing what You want.

I will serve You, God, because You love me. I will serve You by telling others how great You are.

OLD MACDONALD

Traditional
Arr. by Ellen Banks Elwell

vs. 2 ducks; quack-quack
vs. 3 pigs; oink-oink
vs. 4 cows; moo-moo

Old MacDonald

Do you see Mr. MacDonald? Does he live in a big city? Does he live in a little town? Does he live on a farm? How do you know?

"Thank You, God, for my chickens," says Mr. MacDonald. "Thank You for fresh eggs." He likes to feed his chickens. Would you like to help him?

"Thank You, God, for my pigs," says Mr. MacDonald.
Would you like one of his pigs for a pet? What would Mother or Father say about that?

"Thank You, God, for my cows," says Mr. MacDonald.
"Thank You for their fresh milk to drink." Have you thanked God for cows and milk? Will you?

"Thank You, God, for my farm," says Mr. MacDonald. "Thank You for giving me chicks and ducks and pigs and cows. Thank You, God, for being You."

RISE AND SHINE

Spiritual　　　　　　　　　　　　　　　　　　　　　　　　　Arr. by Ellen Banks Elwell

TWINKLE, TWINKLE, LITTLE STAR

Jane Taylor

W. A. Mozart
Arr. by Ellen Banks Elwell

Twin-kle, twin-kle, lit-tle star, how I won-der what you are.

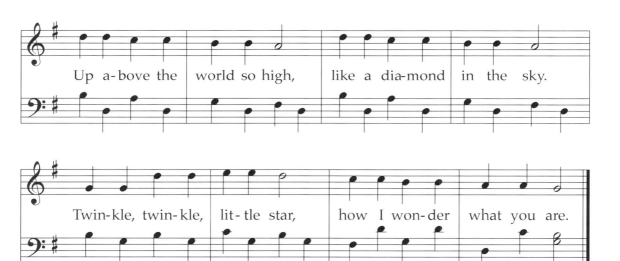

vs. 2
When the blazing sun is gone,
When he nothing shines upon;
Then you show your little light,
Twinkle, twinkle, all the night.
Twinkle, twinkle, little star,
How I wonder what you are.

Twinkle, Twinkle, Little Star

Look! Do you see that pretty star?
It looks like a twinkly diamond.
God made that twinkly star, didn't He?

Look! Do you see the sky
filled with stars?
Did the night put on a dark coat
filled with twinkly little lights?

Look! Do you see that pretty star? Each time you see a star in the sky, say, "Thank You, God, for Your twinkly night lights."

WHO DID?

Traditional

Arr. by Ellen Banks Elwell

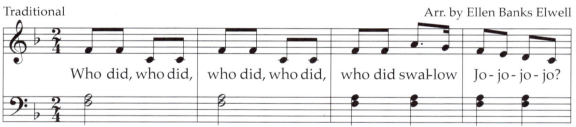

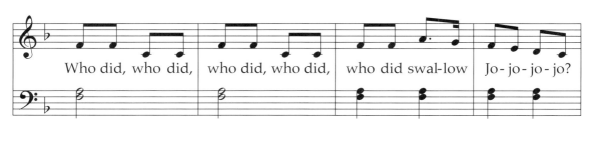
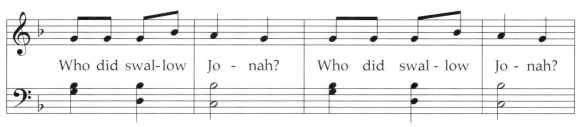
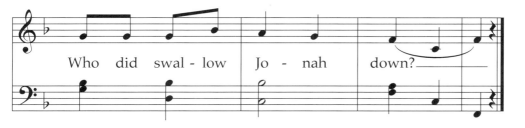

vs. 2
Big fish, big fish, big fish, big fish,
Big fish swallowed Jo-jo-jo-jo . . .
Big fish swallowed Jonah down.

Who Swallowed Jonah?

Who swallowed Jonah from the sea?
Was it a bug, a worm, or a hungry bee?
Do you know?

Who swallowed Jonah,
can you say
If a hippo swallowed
Jonah on that day?
Do you know?

Who swallowed Jonah when he tried to go
On a ship on the sea where the wind would blow?
Do you know?

Who swallowed Jonah, have you heard?
An eagle or a hawk or another hungry bird?
Do you know?

Who swallowed
Jonah—do you
give up?
Did something swallow
Jonah in a great big cup?
Do you know?

MARY HAD A LITTLE LAMB

Sarah Hale
Arr. by Ellen Banks Elwell

Sarah Hale

Ma - ry had a lit - tle lamb, lit - tle lamb, lit - tle lamb.

vs. 2 Everywhere that Mary went . . . the lamb was sure to go.

vs. 3 'Followed her to school one day . . . which was against the rules.

vs. 4 'Made the children laugh and play . . . to see a lamb at school.

vs. 5 Repeat vs. 1

Mary Had a Little Lamb

I love you, little lamb! I love your soft white wool. God gave you that beautiful coat, you know. Thank You, God, for my lamb.

I love you, little lamb! Thank you for going with me when I play. Thank you for going everywhere I go. Thank You, God, for playtime.

I love you, little lamb! Would you like to go to school with me today? We will have fun together. Thank You, God, for school.

I love you, little lamb! My school friends love you, too. Do you see how they laugh and play with us? Thank You, God, that we can laugh.

I love you, little lamb! My friends thank you for playing with them. Thank You, God, for my friends.

I love you, little lamb! It's time to go home now. Do you think Mother will give us a snack? Thank You, God, for everything.

GOD IS SO GOOD

vs. 2 God loves me so . . .
vs. 3 God answers prayer . . .
vs. 4 God is so good . . .

God Is So Good

God is so good.
He gives me a beautiful
world where I can live.
God is so good to me.

God is so good.
He gives me a wonderful
home and family.
God is so good to me.

God loves me so.
He takes care of
me all day long.
God is so good to
me.

God loves me so. He gives me good food and clothing. God is so good to me.

God answers prayer. He listens to me when I talk with Him. God is so good to me.

God is so good.
He gives me His
special Book, the Bible.
God is so good to me.

EENSY WEENSY SPIDER

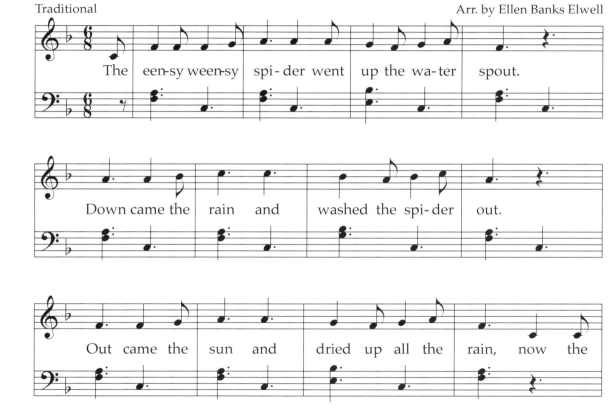

Eensy Weensy Spider

I see an eensy weensy spider.
Do you see it too?
Where is it?

I see a water spout.
The eensy weensy spider sees it too.
What do you think he will do now?

I see a big cloud. The spider doesn't see it. He's inside the water spout. But you see the cloud, don't you?

I see the sun shining.
It will dry up the rain.
It will dry out the water spout.
  Now where is that eensy weensy spider going?

God sends rain. God sends sunshine.
God gives eensy weensy spiders a place to sleep.
Good night, eensy weensy spider.
Good night.

MARY HAD A BABY

Spiritual
Arr. by Ellen Banks Elwell

vs. 2 Where did she lay Him . . .
vs. 3 Laid Him in a manger . . .
vs. 4 What did she name Him . . .
vs. 5 Mary named Him Jesus
vs. 6 Ooh,———

Mary Had a Baby

Look! Do you see the beautiful lady? Her name is Mary. Do you see the little baby? He is Mary's little baby boy.

Where is Mary's baby lying? His bed is not like your bed, is it? His bed is called a manger. Animals ate their food from a manger.

Shhh! Mary's little baby is sleeping.
Do you think that is why the animals are so quiet?

Please don't wake Mary's baby, little lamb.
Please don't wake Mary's baby, little donkey.
Please don't anyone wake Mary's baby.

Look! Mary's baby is waking. Now you can whisper, little lamb. Now you can whisper, little donkey. Now you can whisper too.

"I love You, Baby Jesus," Mary whispers.
Now you know the baby's name. Would you like to say, "I love You Baby Jesus"?

MOZART'S LULLABY

W. A. Mozart
Arr. by Ellen Banks Elwell

Sleep, ba-by, sleep, and good night, all the birds are asleep out of sight.

Qui- et the lambs on the hill. E- ven the bumble-bee's still.

Mozart's Lullaby

It's lullaby time. Shhh. Does someone sing softly to you when it's time to go to sleep?

It's lullaby time.
Shhh. The sky is
falling asleep.
Will you?

It's lullaby time.
Shhh. The bumblebee
is quiet now.
Are you?

It's lullaby time.
Shhh. Don't wake
the man in the moon.
Will you sleep now too?

It's lullaby time.
Shhh. Good night.
Sleep, my little one.
Shhh.

HE'S GOT THE WHOLE WORLD IN HIS HANDS

Spiritual   Arr. by Ellen Banks Elwell

vs. 2 He's got the wind and the rain . . .
vs. 3 He's got the little bitty baby . . .
vs. 4 He's got you and me, brother . . .
vs. 5 Repeat vs. 1

He's Got the Whole World in His Hands

Who sends the wind
through the trees?
God does, that's who.
Thank You, God.

Who sends the rain to water my garden? God does, that's who. Thank You, God.

Who sent our baby into our home?
God did, that's who.
Thank You, God.

Who takes care of me every day? God does, that's who. Thank You, God.

Who watches over you
with loving care?
God does, that's who.
Thank You, God.

Who takes care of our whole wide world?
God does, that's who.
Thank You, thank You, God.

ARE YOU SLEEPING?

French Round　　　　　　　　　　　　　　　　　　　　Arr. by Ellen Banks Elwell

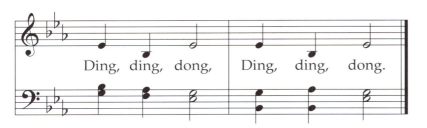

JESUS LOVES ME

Anna B. Warner

William B. Bradbury
Arr. by Ellen Banks Elwell

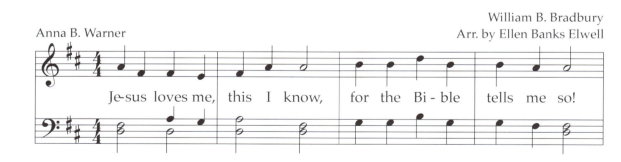

Je-sus loves me, this I know, for the Bi - ble tells me so!

Jesus Loves Me

Shhh! Do you see Jesus?
I think He wants to
whisper something to
me. What do you think
Jesus wants to say?

Shhh! Listen! Do you think Jesus says, "I love you?" Do you think He loves you and me? I think He does.

Shhh! Do you see Jesus? I think He wants to do something special. Do you think He wants to give you and me a special hug?

Shhh! I love You, Jesus. Thank You for loving me too. And thank You for loving other boys and girls.

Shhh! It's time for Mother to read my Bible to me. I love to hear about Jesus. Do you love to hear about Jesus too?

Shhh! My Bible says Jesus loves me. Does your Bible say that too? Thank You, Jesus, for loving me. I love You too.

SIX LITTLE DUCKS

Traditional   Arr. by Ellen Banks Elwell

Six lit-tle ducks that I once knew, fat ducks, pret-ty ducks they were too. But the one lit-tle duck with the fea-ther on his back,

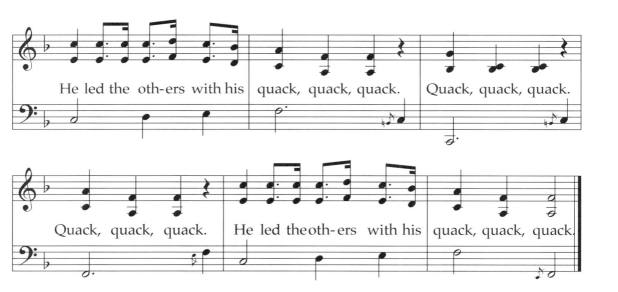

vs. 2 Down to the meadow they would go,
wibble-wobble-wibble-wobble, to and fro,
But the one little duck with the feather on
his back . . .

Six Little Ducks

Which little duck
has a feather on his back?
One little duck goes
QUACK, QUACK, QUACK.

Which little duck
has a feather on his back?
Two little ducks go
QUACK, QUACK, QUACK.

Which little duck
has a feather on his back?
Three little ducks go
QUACK, QUACK, QUACK.

Which little duck
has a feather on his back?
Four little ducks go
QUACK, QUACK, QUACK.

Which little duck
has a feather on his back?
Five little ducks go
QUACK, QUACK, QUACK.

Which little duck
has a feather on his back?
Six little ducks go
QUACK, QUACK, QUACK.

ZACCHAEUS

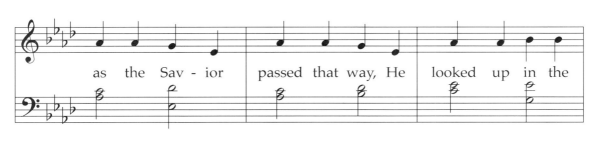

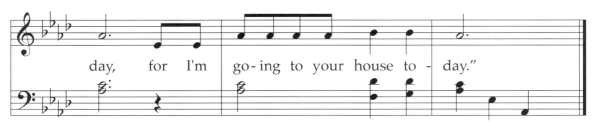

Zacchaeus

Do you see that big crowd? Do you see that little man in the big crowd?
His name is Zacchaeus.

Do you see Jesus? Zacchaeus wants to see Jesus. But he can't. Zacchaeus is too short.

Do you see that tree?
Zacchaeus sees it.
Zacchaeus wants to climb that tree.

Do you see Jesus?
Zacchaeus sees Him now.
Wasn't that a good idea to climb that tree?

Do you see Zacchaeus? Jesus sees him. "Come down," Jesus says. "I want to go to your house."

Do you see Jesus and Zacchaeus?
Zacchaeus wants to be Jesus' friend now.
Jesus wants that too. Aren't you glad?

OH, HOW LOVELY IS THE EVENING
(Round)

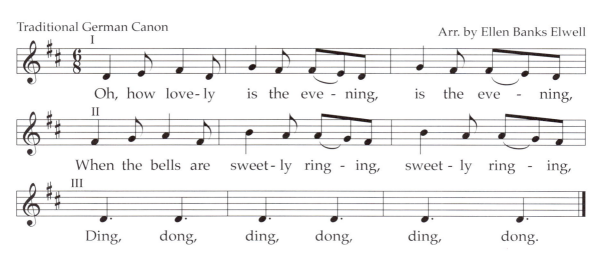

Oh, How Lovely Is the Evening

Why does the sun go down? So you can have a lovely evening. God makes the sunset just for you.

Why does the sky
have so many colors?
So you can have a
lovely evening.
God makes the colors
just for you.

Why does a star
begin to shine?
So you can have a
lovely evening.
God makes the star
shine just for you.

Why do you hear the sound of bells? So you can have a lovely evening. God made your ears just for you.

Why is Mother here with you?
So you can have a lovely evening.
God made your
family just for you.

Why does the whole world seem so beautiful?
So you can have a lovely evening.
God made His world just for you.

ALL THROUGH THE NIGHT

All Through the Night

Look! Do you see the moon in the night sky? I'm glad God made the soft moonlight. I'm glad God made the night.

Look! Do you see the stars in the night sky?
I'm glad God made the twinkly stars.
I'm glad God made the night.

Listen! Do you hear the soft whooo of the owl?
I'm glad God made the soft night sounds.
    I'm glad God made the night.

Listen! Do you hear Mother whisper, "Good night"? I'm glad God gave me a wonderful mother.
I'm glad God made the night.

Oh! Do you feel the softness of your bed? I'm glad God gave me a soft, warm bed where I can sleep.
I'm glad God made the night.

Oh! Do you know that
God is near all night long?
I'm glad God watches
over me tonight.
I'm glad God made the
night.

HERE WE GO 'ROUND THE MULBERRY BUSH

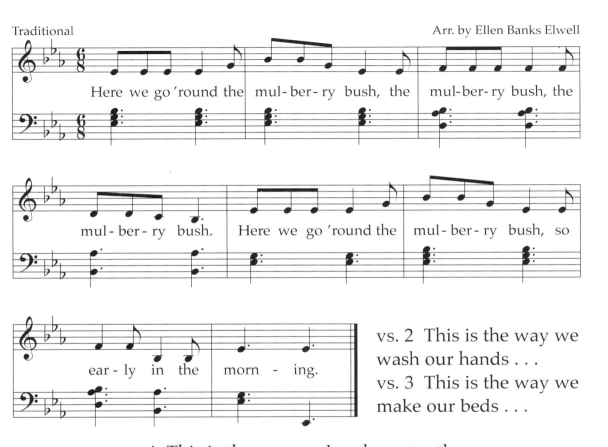

Here We Go 'Round the Mulberry Bush

Good morning, world. It's time to wake up. It's time for me to wake up too. But what shall I do to say "Good morning"?

Good morning, bush. It's time for a wake-up game. My friend and I will hold hands. We will go 'round and 'round. Thank You, God, for fun.

Good morning, hands. It's wash-up time, you know. God wants you and me to be clean. Thank You, God, for clean water so I can have clean hands.

Good morning, bed.
Thank you for
helping me sleep
last night.
Now I'll help
you have a
good day.
Thank You,
God, for
my bed.

Good morning, teeth. Oh, but you feel furry. Thank You, God, for my toothbrush and toothpaste.
They will take that furry feel away.

Good morning, God. I want to go to Your house today. Thank You for Your wonderful house. You'll be there too, won't You?

HALLELU, HALLELU

Traditional — Arr. by Ellen Banks Elwell

Hal-le-lu, hal-le-lu, hal-le-lu, hal-le-lu-jah, Praise ye the

Lord. Hal-le-lu, hal-le-lu, hal-le-lu, hal-le-lu-jah,

LITTLE BOY BLUE

Traditional

Arr. by Ellen Banks Elwell

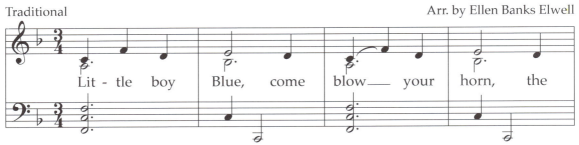

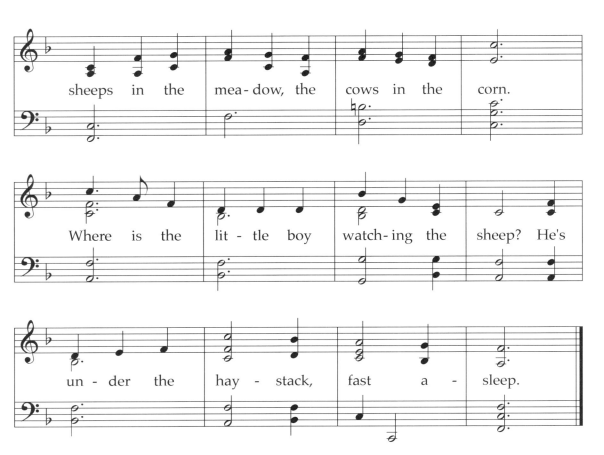

OH, BE CAREFUL

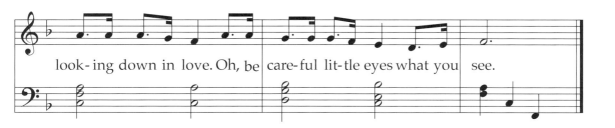

vs. 2 Oh, be careful little ears what you hear . . .
vs. 3 Oh, be careful little mind what you think . . .
vs. 4 Oh, be careful little hands what you do . . .
vs. 5 Oh, be careful little feet where you go . . .

Oh, Be Careful

If Jesus looked with my eyes,
What would He see?
Be careful little eyes
What you see.

If Jesus heard with my ears,
What would He hear?
Be careful little ears
What you hear.

If Jesus thought with my mind,
 What would He think?
  Be careful little mind
   What you think.

If Jesus did things with my hands,
What would He do?
Be careful little hands
What you do.

If Jesus went places with my feet,
 Where would He go?
 Be careful little feet
 Where you go.

If Jesus loved something with my heart,
What would He love?
Be careful little heart
What you love.

I LOVE LITTLE KITTY

I Love Little Kitty

Thank You, God, for kitty.
Thank You that I can
feel her soft fur.
Thank You, God,
for kitty.
Thank You that I can
feel her tongue kiss
my cheek.

Thank You, God,
for kitty.
Thank You that I can
see her play with
some string.

Thank You, God, for kitty.
Thank You that I can see her eat the food I give her.

Thank You, God, for kitty.
  Thank You that I can hear him purr.

Thank You, God, for kitty.
Thank You that I can
take care of her.
Thank You for taking
care of me too.

LITTLE DAVID, PLAY ON YOUR HARP

Traditional
Arr. by Ellen Banks Elwell

Little David, play on your harp, Hal-le-lu, hal-le-lu, Lit-tle Da-vid

play on your harp, Hal-le-lu. Lit-tle Da-vid, play on your

Little David, Play on Your Harp

Once there was a boy named David.
David took care of his father's sheep.
Thank You, God, for taking care of me.

David fought lions and bears.
He would not let them hurt his sheep.
Thank You, God, for keeping
me safe.

David found safe places where his sheep could sleep.
Thank You, God, for my nice house and warm bed.

David told his sheep
how much he loved them.
Thank You, God, for telling me
that You love me.

David sang songs to his sheep.
He praised God, singing and playing his harp.
Thank You, God, that I can praise You too.